FISHING for KIDS

A FAMILY FISHING GUIDE

By Steven A. & Elizabeth May Griffin

The Outdoor Kids Series

FROM

NORTHWORD
PRESS, INC

Box 1360, Minocqua, WI 54548

Library of Congress Cataloging-in-Publication Data

Griffin, Steven A.
    Fishing for kids / by Steven and Elizabeth Griffin.
        p.   cm.
    Summary: Introduces the techniques, equipment, and
bait used to catch various types of fish.
    ISBN 1-55971-145-0 : $7.95
    1. Fishing—Juvenile literature. [1. Fishing.] I. Griffin,
Elizabeth, 1985-   .   II. Title.
SH445.G75   1993
799.1—dc20   92-44448
                                                         CIP
                                                         AC

ISBN: 1-55971-145-0

Edited by Greg Linder
Cover Design by Russell S. Kuepper
Interior Design by Patricia Bickner Linder

Published by: NorthWord Press
                P.O. Box 1360
                Minocqua, WI 54548

For a free catalog describing NorthWord's line of books
and gift items, call 1-800-336-5666.

Printed in U.S.A.

Dedication

To Mary Jo, the authors' wife and mother—
our favorite fishing partner, who always catches
big-enough bass and throws them back.

Cover photo: Robert W. Baldwin
All interior photos by Steven A. and Elizabeth May Griffin except:
Sharon R. Rushton, pp. 4, 62
Courtesy DuPont Stren, p. 12, 72
Tom Huggler, p. 54
Mary Jo Griffin, pp. 6, 61
Dale Smith, p. 74

Art on p. 10 courtesy Wisconsin Department of Natural Resources
Illustrations by Patricia Bickner Linder

Fishing for Kids
Table of Contents

Introduction

How did this father and young daughter write a fishing book? First, we fished. We laughed, we learned, we listened. Then we talked.

Elizabeth, six years old when most of this was written, said many of the things in this book. She told her dad some other things he should talk about. And her dad, Steve, added some thoughts of his own. It turned into this book.

Working together was fun—in the office, and especially when we went fishing. Some days we caught fish. Some days we didn't. We always had fun.

Why fish? Grownups have a harder time answering that than kids do. Big people say it's a game, trying to figure out where to find fish and how to make them bite.

Grownups like to be around lakes, ponds, and rivers. They're glad to be away from work, to take their shoes off, and to dig for worms. Big people like to sit next to a kid and not have to be the boss all the time.

Elizabeth says kids should fish because it's fun: Catching fish. Playing with frogs. Swimming. Camping. Eating the fish. Hiking. Snacking. Getting fish bites. Driving the boat. Playing with the fishing tackle. Catching tadpoles. Getting all excited when the bobber bobs up and down. Seeing animals and birds. Picnicking. Taking friends along. Getting big fish. Writing about fishing.

Steve and Elizabeth with their dog, Buster.

After one fishing trip, Elizabeth wrote this true story in her first-grade classroom at Eastlawn School:

"The Big 'Ol Bass"
By Elizabeth Griffin

My dad and I were fishing.
And when my dad got a bite, he let me reel it in.
My dad got a bite! We traded poles and I reeled it in.
I fought it until it was tired. But I couldn't get it or it would break either the pole or the line.
So my dad had to get in the water.
My dad caught the bass. We saw that the bass had pushed the bluegill (that had first bit the worm) up the line.
We put it in the bucket and got in the car.
My dad got real excited, and I did, too!
And the next day we ate it for dinner.
The end.

We wrote this book hoping it would lead you to fishing stories of your own.

Elizabeth May Griffin
Steven A. Griffin
Midland, Michigan

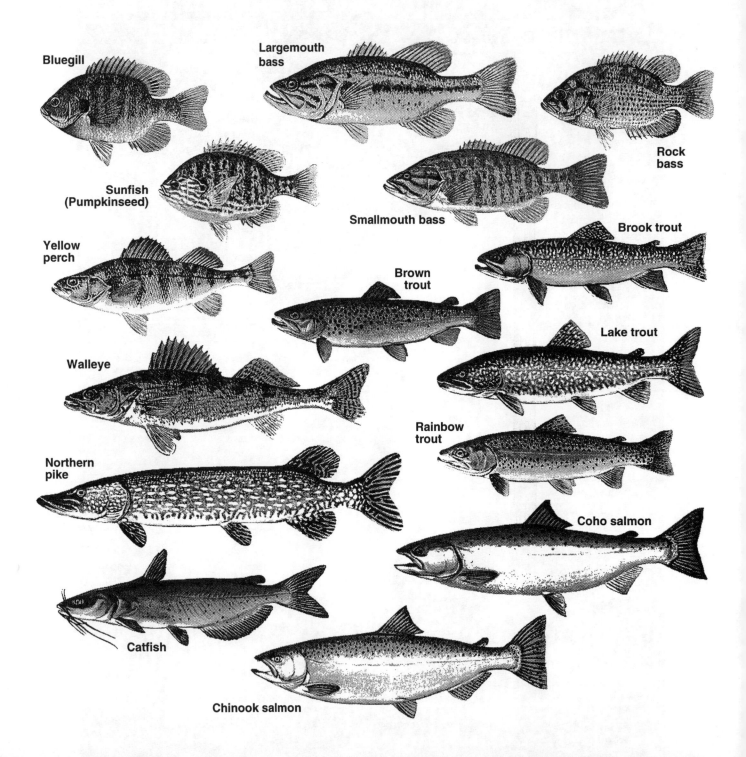

Bluegill

Largemouth bass

Rock bass

Sunfish (Pumpkinseed)

Smallmouth bass

Brook trout

Yellow perch

Brown trout

Walleye

Lake trout

Rainbow trout

Northern pike

Coho salmon

Catfish

Chinook salmon

CHAPTER 1
Meet the Fish

Lots of animals swim. Snakes, frogs, dogs, fish, and even kids swim. But only fish have scales and fins. They live in water; we live in air. To see them, we may have to toss a line into their homes and catch them. Sometimes the fish we catch make a delicious meal. For all these reasons, fish are special.

How would you describe fish? They're animals that live underwater, and they have scales and fins. But what shape are they?

This crappie swims by wiggling its body and tail. The fish uses its fins for balance.

Some fish are shaped like cigars but smell better. Some are shaped like submarines but feel softer. Some are flat and round like cookies, but they're not sweet or crumbly. The fish we catch aren't shaped like fish sticks, or like the fish on your plate at a restaurant. The fish we catch are shaped like fish—kind of oblong with a head and a tail.

Fish are shaped that way for good reasons. A fish doesn't swim like you

A fat largemouth bass moves more slowly through the water than a skinnier fish would.

or me, with arms and legs splashing—or even by moving its fins. The fins mostly help it balance, the same way holding your arms out helps when you're pretending to walk across the high wire.

A fish swims by giving its body, especially its tail, a big wiggle. That wiggle shoots it through the water. You can even try this when you're swimming. Hold your legs together and kick them as if they were your tail. You'll move forward like a fish.

The skinnier the fish is, the faster it can wiggle through the water. Fish like northern pike or walleyes that catch and eat other fish

Hard flaps protect the gills of this steelhead trout.

are skinny and quick. Fish that are more likely to gulp down a frog or a bug—fish like bluegills or bass—are slower and rounder. In fact, bluegills are almost perfectly round.

Fish have mouths and eyes. They have nostrils, too, but they don't breathe air the same way we do. Just about where you'd expect a fish to have ears, it has flaps of hard stuff. When you open these up, you see rows of red things. The red things are called gills. Fish draw water through their mouths and push it out through their gills. The gills remove oxygen from

13

water the same way our lungs remove oxygen from air. Like us, fish need oxygen to live.

A fish smells and tastes what's in the water. The same way the smell of a pizza drifts through the air to your nose, the smell of a leech or some other tasty fish-snack floats through the water to the nostrils of a hungry bass.

You know how you can almost taste a good meal even before it's in your mouth? The fish really does taste the thing it smells when chemicals carried through the water reach special sensors in its mouth and throat. It's as

It's easy to see the lateral lines that run down the side of this brown trout.

14

excited about its meal as you are about yours. In fact, if the fish had a pizza, it sure wouldn't tell the pizza parlor to skip the anchovies. Anchovies are small fish, after all, and most fish like to eat smaller fish.

Fish don't have ears like ours. They have inner ears, located inside their heads. And they have a special hearing system along their sides that's called lateral lines. You can actually see a line of dots on each side if you look closely at a fish. The dots run from behind the gill to just ahead of the tail.

Anything that makes noise underwater—whether it's a swimming fish or a splashing mouse—sends a signal that bumps against these lateral line dots, just as

The scales on this Atlantic salmon are arranged like shingles on the roof of a house, to let the fish slide through the water easily.

if someone was thumping the top of your bicycle helmet. Helmet-thumping probably makes you angry, but the splashing or swimming sounds make a big fish happy: The sounds mean that there's a meal nearby. A little fish uses the same sounds to learn that there's a big fish nearby. Then he hides!

Fish have bony scales on their skin. Scales are hard, flat, and round, like a coin. Some fish, such as trout, have tiny scales. Others, like carp, have scales as big as a quarter. Whatever the size, scales grow a little each year, and scientists can see growth rings on them just like they see rings on a tree. By studying a scale under a microscope, a scientist can count the rings and figure out how old a fish is. You can do that yourself by looking at a scale with a strong magnifying glass or under a microscope.

The spines in the fin on the back of this bluegill can poke a hole in your skin. Handle fish carefully.

The fish's scales overlap each other, like shingles on the roof of a house. They let the fish move smoothly through the water, just as water runs off the roof of your house. If you rub your hand over a fish, it feels smooth when you rub from head to tail, but rough if you rub the other direction.

By the way, if you rub a fish, be careful of the fins. Most fish have fins that fold down against the body, but the fins can also stand up, because they have sharp bones in them called spines. The spines are so hard and sharp they could poke a hole in your skin. Some fish, such as certain catfish, even have special stingers they can use against an enemy. They might think their enemy is you, so be careful when you handle a fish.

CHAPTER 2
Fish Homes

To understand a fish, you need to know where it lives. Some kinds of fish live happily in just about any watery place. Others are very picky. The more you learn about water, the more you'll know about fish. You'll catch more, and maybe you can help protect the water the fish lives in.

Water moves in two ways. We think of wet stuff when we think of water. But when water gets hot and "dries up," it turns into a gas like steam, and that gas floats upward and forms clouds. When the clouds are filled with more water than they can hold, like saturated sponges, they send the water back to earth as rain or snow. So, while a pond may lose water in hot weather, a good rain or a big winter snow will refill it.

Water moves in another way, too. It always wants to go downhill, and the downhill flow eventually leads it to the ocean. Water flows in rivers and creeks. Most ponds and lakes send their extra water into a river or stream. Lakes and rivers hook onto each other, and then one of them hooks onto the ocean, sometimes called the sea.

The sea's water has lots of salt in it, so we call it saltwater. But unless we live next to the sea, the rivers and lakes near us are filled with freshwater, like the water underground or the water in the clouds.

Most fish are built to live in one kind of water or the other. Largemouth bass can only live in freshwater, but mackerel can only survive in saltwater. Since many of us fish mostly in freshwater, most of this book is about catching fish in freshwater creeks, streams, rivers, ponds, and lakes.

If you know where a fish lives, then you'll know where to catch it.

Creeks are about the smallest places you can fish. They're like tiny rivers. The water in some of them comes from glaciers, and from snow that melts in the mountains. Other streams are "fed" by springs, places where underground water bubbles up through the soil.

Streams can be created the same ways, or may form at a spot where two or three creeks meet and share their waters. Rivers are bigger yet: The Mississippi River is a mile wide in some places.

The water in creeks, streams, and rivers is moving. A fish has to swim just to stay in one place. So most fish find places in the river where the the moving water is the slowest. There, they don't have to work so hard.

Watch a river carefully. Not all the water moves at the same speed. If you toss a couple of sticks into different parts of the river, or if you watch leaves float downstream, you'll notice that some parts of the river move faster. In some places, the river will even swirl in a circle, almost like the water in a bathtub when the plug is pulled. Those spots, where the water is waiting its turn to flow downstream, are called eddies.

The waters that move at different speeds are called currents. Often, the best fishing is where two of these currents rub against each other. That's because a fish can rest in a slow current and wait for dinner to come down the express lane!

Underwater, rocks and brush block the water the way a bus shelter blocks the wind. Fish don't ride buses, but they like to wait at a sheltered place for a meal. Fish can be bullies, too. The biggest fish usually gets the best waiting spot. So, if you catch a big fish from one place, the next biggest or toughest fish will probably take that favorite spot. You might catch another big one there later. The spot might become your own special fishing place.

Many exciting fish,
like this steelhead,
swim in rivers.

Fishing off a pier lets you fish in both the shallow and deeper parts of a lake.

Ponds and lakes don't have currents the same way a river does, but fish that live there do find favorite spots. Shallow areas, maybe as deep as you are tall, are home to the smaller fish. Here you'll most often find bluegills, sunfish, and minnows.

Walleyes are happiest in deeper water, and so are trout. Pike and bass go where the food is, so they might be either shallow or deep. The best places to find many of these game fish, which eat other fish, are in spots where both shallow and deep water are nearby. We call a place where shallow water suddenly becomes deeper a drop-off. A big bass or pike calls it a dining room. A game fish can grab a quick meal, if a minnow or another small fish is careless, and after the meal dart back to its cool, deep-water living room in no time at all.

An impoundment, which might also be called a reservoir or flowage, is kind of like a river and kind of like a lake. Impoundments are places where dams have been built on rivers. The dam blocks the water, so the water backs up and covers a lot of land. Eventually it looks like a lake, but the river still flows through it. Fish love impoundments, because they're full of food and fresh water. Fisher-people love impoundments because they're full of fish.

Water always tries to get downhill. That's why it falls over a dam like this one. People find good fishing in the impoundment, a lake formed where water backs up behind the dam. They find good fishing in the river just below the dam, too.

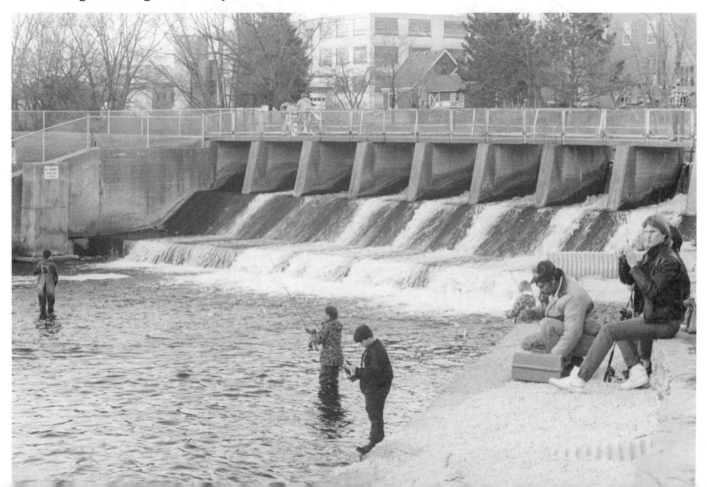

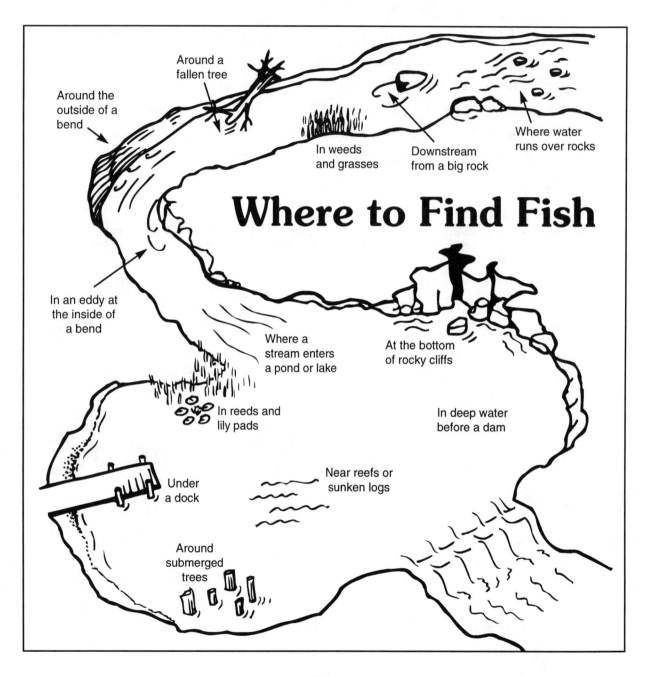

Around a fallen tree

Around the outside of a bend

In weeds and grasses

Downstream from a big rock

Where water runs over rocks

Where to Find Fish

In an eddy at the inside of a bend

Where a stream enters a pond or lake

At the bottom of rocky cliffs

In reeds and lily pads

In deep water before a dam

Under a dock

Near reefs or sunken logs

Around submerged trees

A lake or pond is more than just water with a bottom to it. Weed beds, sunken brush piles, logs, and stumps all make great hideouts for fish. The best panfishers, the people who always seem to catch plenty of sunfish and crappies, fish where there are stumps and brush. One way you can catch more fish is to buy or draw a map of your favorite lake, pond, or river. You can mark places on the map that have good fish-hiding spots and return to those places again and again.

When you think about fish and water, remember that there are two other kinds of water: clean and dirty. Rivers and lakes that are dirty because people have dumped stuff into them are called polluted. Some rivers and lakes are so dirty you can't eat the fish that swim there.

People are trying to clean up polluted waters. You can help by not littering, and by learning all you can about the environment and how to protect it. After all, water's the home of your favorite creatures: the fish!

CHAPTER 3
Fish Habits

Fish don't live alone in a lake or river. They're part of a community, just like you're part of the city, county, or village in which you live. Fish grow up doing "jobs" in their community. A big fish's job may include eating smaller fish. A small fish's job might include being eaten!

Living things eat other living things. We know that, even if we don't think about it very often. A grasshopper eats living green plants. The grasshopper falls into the water and a small fish eats it. Later, a bigger fish eats the small fish. Pelicans like fish, and ospreys and eagles love to eat fish. Otters are good at catching fish, too. And sooner or later, a fox or coyote might eat whatever it was that ate the fish. The whole eating cycle, from the green plants to the coyote, is called a food chain.

There are other food chains, of course. A snail eats plant growth called algae, a duck eats the snail, a fox or a human hunter eats the duck. And there are food chains that lead to you. A bug eats a plant. A minnow eats the bug. A small fish eats the minnow. A big fish eats the small fish. Then you catch the big fish and your family eats it.

Fish are born because mother fish lay eggs and father fish fertilize the eggs. Sometimes mom guards the eggs and the young fish that hatch. Sometimes dad does it. Sometimes nobody watches over them. Nature normally makes sure that enough eggs and baby fish are produced to keep the lake full of fish, even if many of the eggs and little fish quickly become part of the food chain.

To help nature protect the fish in a lake or river, people make rules that tell all

---

A food chain is nearly complete. The minnow ate little organisms. The perch ate the minnow, and the person who caught it might eat the perch.

of us how many fish we can keep, what size they must be, and when and how we can fish for them. You'll find the fishing rules in booklets that you can get at bait and tackle stores or offices of the Department of Natural Resources.

For a fish to hatch and grow, it needs just the right kind of place, known as spawning habitat, for that kind of fish. The bottom and the water must be clean, and there must be hiding spots such as weeds, rocks, or brush, so that young fish can survive. Too often, though, the water is polluted or the bottom cover is pulled out so people can swim there or build cottages.

Clearing out brush, dumping in sand, or draining the water from wetlands makes it easier for people to boat or swim, but harder for fish to raise families. People are getting smarter, though. They're taking better care of fish and fish habitat.

Little fish soon learn to hide. You might see them near stumps and weeds, where they can hide from big fish, seagulls, king-fishers, ospreys, turtles, ducks, and people. As fish get larger, they start to eat bigger things. Instead of

One of our favorite food chain links—a kid eating fresh-fried fish that she caught herself.

If we know what a fish likes to eat, we can offer it a tasty meal.

eating baby foods like tiny bugs and bits of plant, they go after bigger meals such as frogs, minnows, night crawlers, or crayfish.

Sometimes fish eat what's under the water, and sometimes they eat what's on top of the water. They don't have kitchen tables, so they have to eat right where the food is. And what do fish eat? You name it. What they like to eat depends on the kind of fish. Small fish usually like to eat little bugs, algae, plankton, and other tiny living things in the water. Big fish often like to eat little fish.

Some of the things fish eat don't sound very tasty to humans. Rock bass eat worms. Walleyes love leeches. Bluegills crunch on crickets. But all of them like other things, too. Sometimes you like pizza and sometimes you like cookies, right? A fish is sort of like that.

If we know what a fish likes to eat, we can offer it a tasty meal or a snack. Fish spend a lot of their time looking for their next meal, swimming around in a lazy search for something delicious. They do sleep, though, resting without moving.

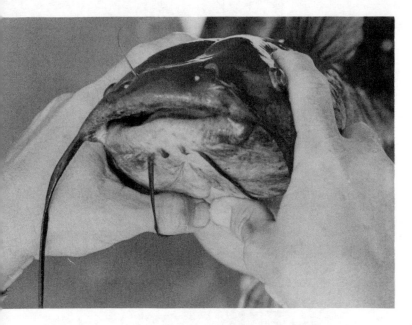

This catfish uses its mouth like a vacuum cleaner to suck food off the bottom of lakes and streams.

And when there's too much noise, or they're full, or there's a bigger fish nearby, they don't mind just hanging around a drop-off, a weed bed, or a sunken log. They feel safe because there's a hiding spot or an escape route nearby.

Most fish don't live a long time—just a few years or so. But some live much longer. Sturgeon, for example, can live 75 years and grow to weigh more than 100 pounds.

Where a fish lives depends partly on what kind it is. The shape of a fish can even give you a clue about where it likes to live. Long, slender fish such as trout, salmon, pike, and walleyes can swim easily. They like swift water, and they might swim hundreds of miles on long rivers.

Chubbier fish such as smallmouth bass can most often be found in slower-moving rivers or in lakes. Fish that are shaped like a flat football, such as bluegills and crappies, usually live in lakes, or in river sections where the water barely moves. And fish whose mouths turn downward like a vacuum cleaner—like suckers, catfish, and carp—will almost always be within a few inches of the bottom, because that's where they find their food. Each fish is perfectly designed for the place in which it lives.

Water can be cold or warm. Some lakes and streams are colder than others.

Even under the ice, fish like this northern pike are still active.

Water temperature depends on many things—where the water comes from, how shaded the shore is, how deep the water is, whether it's muddy or clear, and many other things. But every kind of fish is built to live in water of a certain temperature. Some fish like really cold water, some prefer water that's mildly cold, and some live in warm water. Different people like swimming in different water temperatures, too. Do you like a cold dip on a hot day, or a hot dip on a cold day?

Scientists called fish biologists have learned the temperatures that fish prefer. A lake trout likes very cold, 50-degree (Fahrenheit) water, while bluegills are happiest when it's 68 degrees or so. Of course, fish can survive in colder temperatures, even in winter water that's almost freezing. But the fish may not like it any more than we would!

CHAPTER 4

Big, Little, and In-Between Fish

Some people think there are two kinds of fish. They call little fish "minnows." They call big fish "big fish." But actually there are many kinds of fish, and two fish of the same size can be a different age. For example, an eight-inch salmon is a baby, but an eight-inch bluegill is an old-timer.

Minnows are a kind of fish all their own. They're little when they're young, and they're still little when they're old. Little panfish and game fish, though, are called "fry," or "fingerlings" or just plain "little fish."

Each kind of fish lives a certain way and does a certain job. Each is part of the food chain. Learning what each fish is like and what it does can help you catch it.

Panfish are many people's favorite fish. They swim almost everywhere. They can be caught on almost any tackle, and they're good to eat.

Some people argue about why these fish are called panfish. Is it because they're shaped like a frying pan? Bluegills, sunfish, crappies, and rock bass are shaped that way. But perch aren't. Is it because they're so tasty when you fry them up in a pan? Maybe. Catch some, and decide for yourself.

There are about a zillion kinds of sunfish, or at least it seems that way. Bluegills, sunfish, redears, pumpkinseeds, bream or brim—they're all sunfish. Sunfish are almost round like a coin, if you look at them from the side. And they like all kinds of water—lakes, rivers, and especially ponds.

Some favorite foods of sunfish are worms, insects, grubs (baby bugs that look like worms), and spiders—things you can find in your backyard or in a field.

A young angler admires a bluegill. Bluegills are members of the sunfish family.

Sunfish always seem hungry. And with their flat bodies, they can turn sideways when you have them on the line and fight like a bigger fish.

Crappies are a little more football-shaped than bluegills, but they're still flat and round. There are two kinds—black crappies and white crappies. Both swim in shallow water during spring and fall, and in deeper places during the summer. They eat insects, but they really like small minnows and tiny artificial lures that look like minnows.

This is a black crappie. Crappies like to eat minnows.

Rock bass are chubbier, and they really fight hard when you catch one. They have red eyes, making them easy to identify, and they can't resist a fat, wriggling worm.

Often when someone catches his or her very first fish, it's a yellow perch. These panfish aren't pan-shaped. They look more like a fat cigar or a straight banana, and they have dark stripes on their sides that run from the back to the belly. Perch are not fussy eaters. They'll bite minnows, worms, night crawlers,

A stringer of yellow perch. When they bite, you feel a tug-tug-tug on the line.

crayfish, and many things that seem strange to us, like fish eyes. While other panfish can be found just about anywhere in a lake, perch are almost always right on the bottom. When they bite, you feel a steady tug-tug-tug on the line. And where you catch one perch, others are almost always nearby. They travel in groups of same-sized fish, called schools.

Those are the panfish. Some other fish are called game fish. They don't play games—it's just what people call fish that put up good fights, grow to large sizes, and are good to eat.

Walleyes are favorite game fish. They're relatives of perch—the same shape, but bigger. Sometimes they're more than two feet long. Walleyes' eyes look hazy, but they can see just fine. They like to eat minnows, but they'll gobble a night crawler or a leech if they get a chance. Like perch, they travel in groups, so if you catch one you'll probably catch more nearby.

Largemouth and smallmouth bass are actually relatives of sunfish, but they can grow to more than 20 inches long. Largemouth bass swim in warm lakes and gobble frogs, worms, leeches, minnows, and other living things. Smallmouth bass prefer cool water, and they like to munch on minnows and crayfish.

Northern pike grow big and look mean, maybe because of all the sharp teeth in the pike's mouth. That mouth opens wide, and a pike will eat just about anything that fits inside—sometimes another pike or even a duckling if it gets the chance. People who fish for pike sometimes use a wire leader—a piece of strong wire between the fishing line and the hook—to keep the fish from biting through the line or tearing through it with its teeth. Keep your hands away from those sharp teeth, but otherwise you don't have to worry about a pike biting you.

Smallmouth bass like these, and largemouth bass too, can grow to be more than 20 inches long.

Trout are also game fish. They live in many places, and they're all streamlined in shape, long and thin. Rainbow trout have colored stripes along their sides, like a

36

Trout are game fish that live in many places.

faint rainbow where the lateral lines are. Brown trout have brown dots on their sides. Brook trout are bright, with red, yellow, and white spots, and orange bellies. Their backs are covered with dark, wormy-shaped markings. Lake trout have forked tails and dark squiggles on their back like brook trout.

Trout in streams and rivers like to rest where a log or other cover protects them from the current and from their enemies, just like you might hide behind a tree to dodge the wind or play hide-and-seek. In lakes, trout like to hide in deep water.

37

White suckers like these are sometimes called rough fish. But they have important jobs to do, and if they're caught in clean water, they're tasty.

A worm, a minnow, or a lure might catch you a brown, brook, or rainbow trout. In small lakes, one of those baits or a marshmallow or even a kernel of corn might convince a trout to bite. On big lakes—*really* big lakes—people sometimes drive their boats around and pull baits or lures along behind them. The fish has to catch the moving bait.

Some people call suckers, carp, catfish, and others "rough fish." Others call them "trash fish," but they have important jobs to do. They eat small things in the water, leaving it cleaner. They also eat fish, insects, and other things. Some rough fish are really good to eat, as long as they come from clean water. And they can all put up a good fight, so it's fun to try to catch one, even if you don't eat it.

A sucker has a round mouth that faces downward, so it can slurp food from the bottom of the lake or stream. Carp are big, with big scales. Catfish, including bullheads, have whiskers that look like they might have come from a real cat.

Any of the rough fish will bite worms or night crawlers, and some people who really like these fish put together special baits that stink—unless you're a catfish or a sucker or a carp, in which case you think the baits smell just fine.

You might be able to catch other fish where you live: coho or chinook salmon, striped bass, or pickerel. Take the time to learn which fish are your neighbors. You'll catch more fish, and you'll have more fun when you know just what you're after.

Using a guidebook is a good way to identify the fish you catch.

39

CHAPTER 5

From Hooks to Baits

A fishing store or catalog is full of fishing stuff. More stuff than you could carry. More than you could use. More than you could afford. And much more than you need.

To catch a fish, you don't need much equipment. A hook and a line will do it. You can even use a bent pin or a safety pin for the hook and a string for your fishing line. But a few things made just for fishing will help you a lot. We call those things tackle.

The most important piece of equipment is the hook. It's the simplest, and it costs the least, too. A simple hook is really just a wire shaped like the letter "J." At the top end is a loop, and you can tie your fishing line onto the loop. At the short end of the hook is a point and something called a barb. The barb is the sharp little tab that you wouldn't find on a letter "J." It holds the hook in place once the fish has taken the point in its mouth. The barb latches onto the fish's mouth easily, but won't back out so easily.

That's how a simple hook works. But there are many types of hooks. Some are double or triple, with more than one "J" hook welded together. Some are smaller than a pencil eraser. Some are as big as your hand. Some are attached to artificial lures—things made of plastic, metal, or other material to look like food that a fish might want to eat. Some hooks are made especially to hold minnows and night crawlers.

A fishing store has more fun fishing equipment than you could carry.

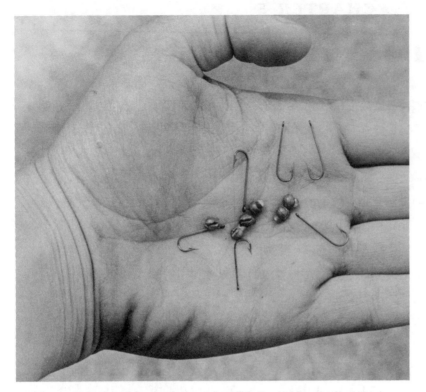

Here are some light hooks and a few sinkers. With these and a little fishing line, you can catch a fish.

Which hook is best? That depends. To catch big fish, you can use a big, strong hook. But a small fish has a small mouth. You'll do better catching smaller fish if you use a small hook.

Hooks must be sharp so they'll hold onto fish. If you keep getting bites but the fish are getting away, it might be time to sharpen your hook. Pulling the point of the hook across a small file will help.

Hooks can get bent out of shape, too—sometimes they're bent when a big fish bites. You can bend them back into shape with a pair of pliers.

Be careful with hooks. You can hook yourself instead of a fish, or you might hook someone near you. Being hooked hurts, and you don't want to end your fishing trip by heading for a doctor's office to have the hook removed. If you hook yourself, be sure to tell an adult and have the wound treated so it won't get infected.

Most fishing is done with monofilament line. That's a clear, plastic-like string.

It's measured by how easily it breaks. The higher the "pounds-test" number on the package, the stronger the line is. Fishing line that's two-pound test is thin and breaks easily. Six-pound test is medium-strong. Ten-pound test is strong enough for really big fish.

You might think you'd want the strongest line you could find. But the stronger the line, the thicker it is. It's harder to tie knots in thick line, and thick line is harder to cast. It's also easier for fish to see thick line—and if they see your line, they probably won't bite your hook. You can catch a 15-pound fish on 10-pound test line. You just have to be careful not to pull too hard, or your line will break.

For most fishing, line rated at six or eight pounds is good. If you're not sure what kind of line you should use, ask someone who knows about the lake or river where you'll be fishing, and knows which fish swim there.

For a reel to work well, it must be filled with plenty of good fishing line. If your casting is awful, maybe you need new line on your reel. To keep your line in good shape longer, don't store your rod and reel where it will get too hot, or where lots of sunlight will hit it. Too much heat or sunlight weakens the line. Basements, closets, or garages are usually good. Cars are bad, because sunlight comes through the windows.

You can use many different knots to tie your fishing line to the hook. A good one is the "clinch knot." To tie a clinch knot, thread your line through the eye, or the hole, of the hook. We call the line that hasn't been through the hook the "standing" line, and the piece that has already gone through the hook the "tag" end.

Wrap the tag end around the standing line about five or six times, and make each wrap a little farther from the eye of the hook. Now poke the tag end through the opening between the hook eye and the first wrap. Wet the line a little

CLINCH KNOT

Thread your line through the eye, or the hole, of the hook. Wrap the end around the line about five or six times. Then poke the end through the opening between the hook eye and the first wrap.

Wet the line a little (spit works), hold the tag end, and slowly pull the main line. The knot should look neat and tight. Trim off the end.

Here's how to tie a clinch knot.

(spit works), hold the tag end, and slowly pull the main line. The knot should look neat and tight. Otherwise, try again. Be patient. It takes practice to become a good knot-tier, but it's worth it.

Sinkers do just what they say. They make the line and the bait sink all the way down to where the fish are. There are many types of sinkers. Most of them can either be pinched onto the line or tied onto it. It's fun to collect different sizes and shapes of sinkers.

Of all the sinkers, the most common is the split-shot, which pinches onto the line. Split-shots are round lead balls with a slice cut in one side. You thread your fishing line into the slot, then pinch the ball closed with pliers. You can add one shot at a time until there's enough weight to hold the bait on the bottom or to hold the bobber down.

For fishing right on the bottom of the river or lake, you might use a tie-on sinker. These are shaped like eggs or teardrops, or even diamonds, with wire loops onto which you can tie the fishing line.

Usually you'll place a sinker on the line between you and the hook. When you use a bobber, the sinker is between the bobber and the hook, usually six to 12 inches above the hook. Sometimes, though, you may want the sinker right on the

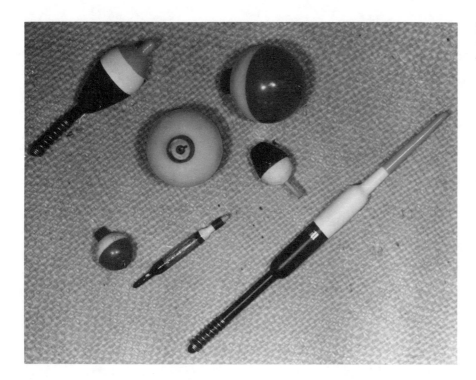

Bobbers come in all shapes and sizes.

bottom and the hook up higher. A sinker with a ring on it works well. The hook and bait float up from the bottom, but the sinker keeps them from floating too high.

Bobbers do two things. They hold the bait off the bottom, and they tell you when you're getting a bite. Bobbers come in all shapes and sizes. Two major kinds are round bobbers and stick bobbers. Others are in-between. Whatever the type and whatever the size, they all bob on the water where you can see them. When you can't see your bobber, it's probably underwater—and that usually means a fish is chomping your bait.

Sometimes the bobber will go underwater and come back up, or maybe it'll just wiggle a little. Later, when you crank in your line, you may find that a fish has shortened your worm or even eaten it! Watch your bobber carefully. It'll tell you when there's a fish interested in your bait.

You can use all kinds of baits for fishing. Some of them are things that a fish eats every day. Others are things—weird things, really—that fish will try to eat.

45

(There are also metal or plastic things called lures that are made to look like good fish foods. We'll talk about them in the next chapter.)

Which baits should you use for fishing? How about these:

Fish and Foods

Here's a list of fish and some of the foods they like:

THE FISH	THE BAIT
Bass (largemouth, smallmouth)	minnows, worms, insect larvae, frogs, crayfish
Bluegills	worms
Carp	worms, doughballs
Catfish	worms, stinkbait
Crappies	small minnows, insects
Northern pike	minnows
Perch	minnows, insects, worms, crayfish
Sunfish	worms, grubs, insects, spiders
Trout (brook, brown, rainbow)	worms, minnows, grasshoppers, marshmallows, corn
Walleye	minnows, leeches, nightcrawlers

An all-time favorite bait for all kinds of fish is a night crawler or other worm. One wriggle from a worm and the fish thinks, "Hmm—a tasty breakfast." The fish bites the worm, gets hooked, and you catch him. Now maybe *you've* got a tasty breakfast.

A nightcrawler threaded on a hook makes a great bait.

Another nice thing about worms is that you can find them yourself. With permission, dig in a garden spot and see how many worms and crawlers you find in the dirt. Night crawlers also come out at night on lawns, and sometimes after a rain you can spot them on the sidewalk or under a pile of damp leaves.

Once you've found them, night crawlers and worms must be kept cool and damp. Don't make them *too* wet, though, or they'll drown. Shredded newspapers make good bedding for them. They're sensitive to light, so keep them in the dark, too. A shady garage is a good place to keep a foam box or a can of worms or

A minnow can be hooked through the top of its back.
This angler is using a treble (or triple-pointed) hook.

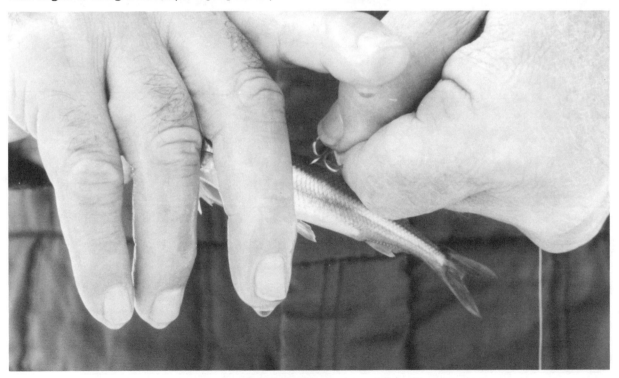

night crawlers until you're ready to use them.

Crawlers and worms are usually threaded onto a hook with a little piece left dangling off the end of the hook. Cover as much of the hook as you can with the crawler or worm.

Another favorite bait is a minnow. You usually have to buy minnows, although in some places you can put a trap baited with oatmeal flakes in the lake to catch your own, or use a long net to trap them. Minnows must be kept cool, with plenty of fresh water. When you're ready to fish, try hooking a minnow through the lips, or through the top of the back just under the fin, so it can swim around.

Marshmallows are good fish baits. Some are made just for fish, but if you use people marshmallows you can eat some of them. Just be sure you have enough left to fish with. Other good fish baits include grubs, crickets, grasshoppers, packaged dead minnows (sold in jars), salmon eggs, cheese, corn, and balls of bread dough.

Different fish like different foods, and learning which fish likes which foods is fun. Try different baits until you find one that's your favorite. Or, better yet, use the one your favorite fish likes best.

CHAPTER 6

Fishing, Filleting, and Frying

There are two main ways of fishing. You can cast a line out and pull it back in slowly, a little at a time. Or you can toss out a bait and let it sit there while you relax. Either way, you need to get your bait or lure to the fish.

There are all sorts of ways to reach fish. Some people just use the string or line without a pole, and toss the bait out from the shore or lower it from a boat. That's hard to do, though.

A simpler way to fish is by using a cane pole. These are long sticks, two or three times as tall as you are. The line is tied to the top of the pole. On the line is the bobber, the sinker, the hook, and the bait. You swing the pole backward then forward, so the line swings out over the water. With a little practice, you can make the bait splash down right where you want it. When the fish bites, you use the pole to lift the fish out of the water. It's a fun way to fish.

Sooner or later, most people want to fish with a rod and reel. These let you cast farther, and they help you reel a fish in if you hook one. There are several kinds of reels, with rods to match.

Many fishers find that the spincast outfit is perfect for their needs. A spincast reel is closed, which means that most of the moving parts are covered up and you can't see much of the line. The only time you see the line is when it comes out of the cap of the reel. A big push-button on the back of the reel releases the line so you can cast it.

Most people enjoy fishing with a rod and reel.

CASTING WITH A SPINCAST REEL

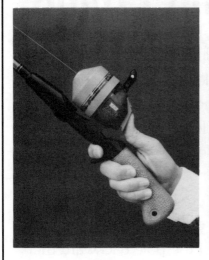  

To cast, hold the spincast rod and reel in one hand with the reel upward. With your thumb, push the button down and hold it down. Swing the rod back, then forward again. At about the time the rod points slightly forward, let go of the button. The lure or bait should fly gently toward the spot you're aiming at.

It should. But sometimes it doesn't. Practice can help. Try practicing your casting in a yard or at a park, using a practice plug or lure with the hooks removed so you don't catch a person instead of a fish. Casting toward a target, such as a big circle on the ground, helps you improve.

You may have seen rods and reels made especially for kids. They're only a couple of feet long, and sometimes they have pictures of cartoon characters on them. They're great for new fishers, especially if you're fishing from a dock or boat and dropping the bait straight down into the water. But for casting, you'll have

CASTING WITH A SPINNING REEL

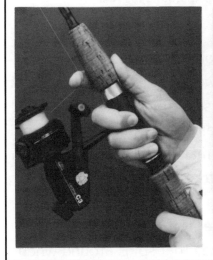  

better luck with a longer rod. (Sometimes the reel from a small rod can be attached to a longer rod.)

Spinning rods and reels take some getting used to. Spinning reels hang below the rod, and you can see all the line wrapped around the reel. A metal arm, called a bail, catches the line and wraps it onto the spool when you reel.

To cast, pinch the line against the rod handle with a finger, then flip the bail. Pull the rod back and, just when you'd lift your finger off the spincast reel button, lift your finger off the line to release it.

There are also baitcast and fly fishing rods and reels. They take more training. The ones we've described are a lot of fun, and you can try one of the more complicated outfits later.

Fishing with bait is fun. You get lots of bites. But fishing with lures is fun, too.

This angler is using a spinning reel. You can see the line wrapped around his reel.

Lures are objects made of plastic, metal, or wood. They're made to look or act like something that a fish would eat. You cast them out and reel them back in to make them move like a fish or some other critter. Here are some of the lures you can try:

A spinner is a lure with a teardrop-shaped blade that spins around when it's pulled through the water.

Spoon lures were first made from real spoons. Now they're made just for fishing, and they wobble when you reel them in. Their shininess attracts fish.

Plugs are made of wood or plastic, and they're built to look or act like real fish. Some plugs float, some sink, and some float until you start reeling them in, when they dive below the water. Some look exactly like real fish, and others are built to wobble like a real fish would if it was trying to get away.

Jigs are hooks with a painted blob of lead on them. Sometimes they have an extra dressing made of feathers, plastic, or other material. They sink quickly, and you can fish with them by reeling them in slowly. You can use jigs just the way they

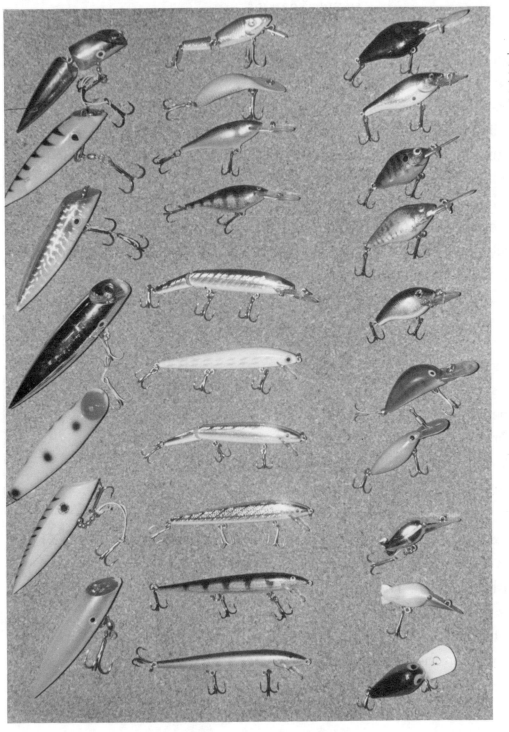

Plugs are built
to look or act
like little fish.

are, or you can add bait or plastic lures. People sometimes say that adding bait "sweetens" the hook.

Plastic lures are soft copies of minnows, night crawlers, crayfish, or other baits. They look just like the real thing, except they come in colors that you'd never see swimming around in your favorite lake. We call them lures because we hope they'll "lure" the attention of a big, hungry fish.

When you first start fishing, you probably won't have a lot of equipment. You can keep your supplies in a little box or bag. But after a while, your collection of fishing stuff will grow. There are hundreds and hundreds of fishing things you can collect and try out. Here's a checklist of things to bring along when you go fishing:

Fishing Gear

☐ Fishing rod   ☐ Life jacket   ☐ Bait

☐ Hooks   ☐ Tackle box   ☐ Fishing hat

☐ Bobbers   ☐ Food for snacks   ☐ Sunscreen

☐ Sinkers   ☐ A bucket or stringer   ☐ Sunglasses

☐ Pliers   ☐ Fishing rules and regulations booklet

☐ First aid kit   ☐ This book!

A tackle box is handy for keeping all your stuff in one place, so it won't get lost and can't hook anyone. A tackle box with ruler markings makes it easy for you to measure the fish you catch. There are rules about how long some kinds of fish must be before you can keep them.

Don't forget to close and latch your tackle box. That keeps the sun from shining too brightly on the stuff inside, and maybe melting it. If the tackle box is

This metal stringer will keep the smallmouth bass from getting away.

latched and somebody knocks it over, your fishing stuff will stay inside the box.

If you fish with a bobber and bait, you can watch the bobber for a sign of a bite. Without a bobber, whether you use bait or a lure, you have to feel the bite. That's not hard with a moving lure. There's a sudden tugging on the line as you reel the lure in.

Sometimes the line stops coming in, and there's no fish on the hook. You're probably hooked on the bottom. A weed on the bottom pulls the line down and holds it there, but a fish will pull the line away from you. It takes practice to be able to tell the difference. But in fishing, practice is a big part of the fun.

Sometimes you can trick fish by reeling in your line a little at a time. The fish think your worm is wiggling away. If you make the pole and line shake, it makes the worm shake. That excites the fish and it attacks, the way your cat pounces on a jiggling piece of yarn. Sometimes, though, your cat isn't interested. Sometimes the fish isn't. You can tell when you have a bite because the tip of your rod is tugged downward. It bounces because the fish is pulling on it.

What should you do when you get a bite? Give the rod a jerk to make sure the fish is hooked. We call that "setting the hook." Now keep the line tight and win the tug-of-war to catch your fish.

A small fish can be cranked right in by turning the reel handle. If it's a big fish, you might notice that you're cranking the handle but no line is coming in. Wait for the fish to tire out. A really big fish might pull line off the reel whether you're cranking or not.

Take your time. Enjoy the fight. Keep the line tight, so the hook can't fall out of the fish's mouth, and keep reeling line onto the reel when you can. But wait for the fish to get tuckered out. Then you can slide the fish onto the shore if it's a small one, or lift it into your boat or onto the pier.

A bigger fish, or a toothy one like a pike, or one with stingers like a bullhead catfish can best be captured with a landing net. Slide the net into the water, then pull the fish into it with your line. You can lift the net with the fish inside it and get it onto shore or into your boat.

Holding a fish is tough. They're slippery, and they have sharp spines in their fins. Carefully grip the fish while smoothing down the fins from front to back. Then use pliers to gently wiggle the hook loose. Take a good look at the fish. What kind is it? What makes it so beautiful?

Now decide whether you want to keep it or not. Check the rule book to make sure the fish is long enough, then either turn it loose or put it on a stringer or in a fish basket. A stringer is like a leash that holds fish by the lip. A fish basket is a wire cage for holding your catch. Both allow the fish to swim in water without getting away.

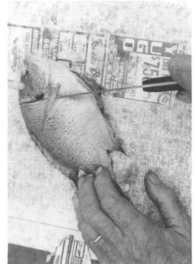

Scaling and gutting a fish is the simplest way to prepare it for cooking.

Some people kill the fish they're going to keep by thumping them on the head with a stick, then putting the fish in a cooler packed with ice. You'll want to keep the fish either alive or cold until you're ready to prepare them.

When you've caught a few fish, you may start thinking about a fish fry. But first you have to clean your fish, so they're just right for cooking. Be sure to ask an adult to help you.

There are two simple ways to clean fish. Rubbing a knife or a fish scaler from the tail toward the head will peel off the scales. They'll go flying, so do it over an old newspaper. When you've removed the scales from both sides, carefully cut the belly open. Then cut off the fish's head, just behind the gills. The fish's insides can be pulled out. Rinse the fish, then it's ready for frying.

Some people fillet their fish. That means they cut off the big flaps of meat on each half of the fish and throw away the rest. To fillet a fish, start by carefully cutting downward along the backbone from the gills to the tail. Do this a few times, and cut a little deeper each time until you reach the rib cage. Now cut a line behind the gill, like you were starting to cut off the head. Peel the meat away from the bones, and cut off the flap of meat with the skin still attached. Lay the meat skin-down on the newspaper. Slide your knife between the skin and meat, and wiggle it forward. When you're done, you can lift the meat off the skin. Rinse the meat, and it's ready to fry.

Fish can be rolled in a batter, such as pancake flour, then placed in a frying pan with hot grease. Cook the meat until it's brown on both sides. Carefully remove it and let the oil drain for a minute onto a paper towel. Then eat!

When filleting a fish, cut away the big slabs of meat from each side of the fish, then peel the skin away from it.

Fresh-caught fish for lunch!

Whole fish are full of bones, so chew carefully when you're eating one. Even a filleted fish should be chewed carefully, in case you missed a few bones.

What happens next? Go out tomorrow, if you can. Repeat what you did today. Keep casting, and you'll catch yourself more fish!

CHAPTER 7

Fishing Safety

People who love to fish think fishing is more fun than just about anything else. But they know fishing can be dangerous if they're not careful. You'll need to learn how to fish safely, and what to do if trouble comes.

The first rule of safe fishing is never to fish alone or without permission. Make sure there's someone nearby who can help you if you're in trouble, and don't wander off while you're fishing. You might get lost.

One of the best things about fishing is being near the water. But if you fall in and can't get out, you could drown. So if you're going to spend time around the water, it's important to learn how to swim. There are classes for every age and ability, and you can even learn how to save others who are in trouble. Swimming is a fun sport and a great way to stay in shape. And it's an important part of safe fishing.

Even if you know how to swim, there are times when swimming is difficult or impossible. Maybe the water's too cold. Maybe you're too tired to swim, or you've hurt yourself. That's why people wear life jackets, or what some call personal flotation devices (PFDs). These look like the fluffy, warm vests that people wear in winter, but they're filled with foam or some other lightweight material that floats. If you fall into the water, the light stuff in the vest helps you stay afloat. Life jackets made with foam cost a little more, but they stay in good condition longer.

Life jackets come in several sizes. A vest only helps you if it's the right size and style—and if you're wearing it when you need it. If you wore your dad's shoes,

---

The first rule of safe fishing is never to fish alone or without permission.

they'd probably fall off when you tried to walk in them. It's the same way with a life jacket. Wearing an adult vest won't work because it may slip off if you fall into the water.

Life jackets are made in kids' sizes, and some even have cartoon characters or other designs on them. Get one, keep it in good shape, and wear it whenever you're fishing. When you put on the vest, tighten the straps so they're snug but comfortable. If you happen to fall in, even if you're not able to swim, the vest will hold your head and face above the water.

Fair is fair, right? If kids have to wear life vests,

A life jacket is a great safety measure. It lets you relax and enjoy the fishing.

adults should, too. Some adults don't wear PFDs, even though they'll probably admit that they should. Wear yours, and try to convince your adult fishing partner to wear one. Some adult life jackets are even built like fishing vests, with pockets to hold tackle and other stuff. They're handy, and they can save a life.

The sun can warm you up when you're fishing, but it can also cause trouble if it's bright and you're outdoors long enough to get a sunburn.

Sunscreens are lotions that keep the sun from burning bare skin. The higher the number on the bottle, the more the lotion protects you. Use a sunscreen with a rating of at least 15, and don't stay outside for very long if your skin feels hot. Some of the suncreens have protection numbers as high as 45. If you have light-colored skin and you sunburn easily, one of those might be good. There are even sunscreen lotions made with special smells so that, if you touch your lure or your bait, the smell will attract fish instead of scaring them away. Other sunscreens are waterproof, so they'll stay on if you're swimming and fishing.

Sunglasses keep your eyes from getting tired. They also shield your eyes from harmful ultraviolet rays that come from the sun, and they can protect your eyes from hooks, sinkers, bugs, and other flying objects. You can ask a salesperson for "shades" that block ultraviolet (UV) rays and have impact-resistant lenses, which means they're harder to break.

Another way to protect yourself from the sun (or rain or bugs) is by wearing a fishing hat. Some people like baseball caps, some like floppy hats, some even like cowboy hats. A good one fits tightly

A fishing hat protects your head and face from the sun. Sunscreen and long sleeves help protect you, too.

so the wind won't blow it off, but still feels comfortable. That's what you need in a fishing hat.

Bug lotion can keep mosquitoes, ticks, and black flies away. Some lotions are made just for kids. Ticks, in particular, can make you sick, even though they're only about as big as the period at the end of this sentence. If you have a tick on you at the end of the day, tell an adult.

First aid means taking care of injuries where they happen, so that you're okay until you can get to a doctor's office. Schools, scout groups, and Red Cross chapters offer classes in first aid. Taking a class and carrying a good first aid kit means you can take care of little problems before they turn into big ones. It's a good idea to keep a small first aid kit with a few bandages and first aid cream in your tackle box.

The best way to fish safely is to avoid problems in the first place. Always be careful of fish hooks. They're sharp, and they can poke through your skin. Casting is dangerous if you don't pay close attention when you're making your casts. Never cast your line in anyone else's direction, because you might injure them.

When you're outdoors, don't eat wild plants unless an adult checks them and makes sure that they're edible. Even then, keep a sample of what you ate in case it makes you sick. The sample could help a doctor treat your illness.

A nature book can help you learn to identify plants that you should stay away from. Poison oak, poison ivy, stinging nettle, and other plants can scratch you, give you a rash, or sting you. It's easier to avoid them than it is to treat the itchy problem on your skin.

When you're fishing in a boat, safety is extra important. Never stand up when you're in a canoe or a small boat, because it could tip over. Sit in the middle of the boat if there's no one next to you. And move around quietly, so you don't spook the fish.

Shorelines and docks are great places to fish, but they can be dangerous, too. Don't fish anyplace where the bank is so steep or the dock is so high that you can't climb back up if you fall in the water. And above all, be sure to wear your life jacket.

Docks and piers are great places to fish, but safety is important here, too.

Safety even includes your snacks. Make sure anything that might spoil—chicken, potato salad, and foods like that— is kept cool until you're ready to eat it. If you're cooking your lunch, ask an adult to help you, and be careful around the campfire.

Here's the best news of all: If you're careful when you're fishing, you'll easily avoid most problems and you'll be able to solve the others. You'll spend most of your time having fun and catching fish!

CHAPTER 8

Fishing Manners

Having good fishing manners really means having respect—for fishing rules, for the fish, for nature, and for other people.

People make fishing rules so that everyone has a chance to fish. The rules also make sure people don't catch so many fish today that there aren't enough left for tomorrow or next year.

One of the rules is that most older kids and adults need to buy a fishing license, or permit, if they want to fish. The money that's paid for fishing permits is used to keep waters clean, to raise more fish, or to create new places to fish. Most people who fish are proud that they chip in to help pay for their fun.

Other fishing rules tell you when and where you can fish, and how many fish you can keep. There are rules for how big some fish must be before you can keep them. To follow the rules, you'll need to learn how to tell the kinds of fish apart, and how to count and measure them. But that's how you can help take care of our fish.

Many people like to eat some of the fish they catch. Fish meat is delicious, and it's fun to sit down to a meal that you caught yourself. But it's also fun to catch fish and release them so that you (or someone else) can catch them again another day. If you don't think you'll be having a fish fry soon, carefully put the fish back in the water.

Whether you keep a fish or release it, you'll probably have to touch it. That can be a little scary, because the fish has those sharp, bony fins. If you grab a bass by

---

Part of being a good angler is catching fish. The other part is having respect for other people and for nature.

the lower jaw (being careful of the hooks!), it will quit flopping. Don't try that with pike or walleye, though, since they have sharp teeth. It's a better idea to hold those fish behind the head. You can hold a panfish around the middle, but first you have to slide your hand over it from front to back to smooth down the fins.

If you're going to release a fish, touch it only with wet hands. That way you

If a fish is too small or the wrong kind, or if you're not going to have a fish fry, you can release it gently.

won't disturb the "fish slime," a coating of mucus that actually protects the fish from disease and bacteria. If possible, keep the fish in the water while you gently work the hook loose with pliers or a hook-removing tool.

Part of good manners is not making a mess. After you've left your fishing spot, no one should be able to tell you've been there. Don't leave any clues behind. You can leave the lake and your fishing spot as clean as it was when you came—maybe even cleaner. That's how you can show your respect for nature.

Good manners includes recycling, too. One of the best ways to recycle things is to reuse them. You can store food, bait, and other stuff in containers that you use again and again. Butter tubs, plastic peanut butter jars, and other unbreakable food containers can be washed out carefully and used to hold snacks, hooks and sinkers, or night crawlers. (Be sure you know which is which!) A bread bag or a paper sack can be used to carry home your trash and maybe some litter that someone else left behind.

Keeping the land clean is important. So is keeping the water clean. When you wash, do it far away from the lake or river, carrying water to your clean-up spot. If you have to go to the bathroom outdoors, walk away from the water—farther than you can throw a stone—and find a spot where you're out of sight. Nature puts plenty of bugs in the soil, and these bugs go to work turning your waste material into more soil.

Having good manners means respecting wildlife and plants. Be sure to leave young animals alone, because you might injure them. And a creature's mother, trying to protect her young, might come after you! So watch wildlife from a safe, respectful distance.

It's not a good idea to pick wildflowers. If too many of them are picked, they won't be able to sow enough new flower seeds. Many are endangered species,

Catch an adult to fish with you!

and picking them could hurt their chances for survival. You can enjoy looking at them as a bonus to your fishing.

Having good manners means respecting other people, too. Give other people plenty of room to fish in, and don't crowd them if they have a good fishing spot.

72

Make room for other fishers, and try not to make a lot of noise. Noise can scare the fish or bother other people.

You can share the fun of fishing by inviting friends, neighbors, and even brothers or sisters to fish with you. Don't forget to catch an adult to be your fishing partner. If you help your favorite adult get things done around the house, he or she will have more fishing time. You can also help gather the fishing tackle and prepare the fishing snacks.

One way to have more fun fishing is to learn more about the outdoors. People who fish learn to read nature's signs. For example, a red-winged blackbird on cattails might tell you where there's a big bass. Minnows jumping out of the water might mean there's a big fish chasing them. Changes in the clouds can tell you what kind of weather is coming.

Take nature books along with you when you fish. A bug cage or a magnifier can give you a closer look at small living things. If you don't have a book with you, draw a picture of any new creature you see. You can look it up later at home or at the library and find out what it is. You can also learn about fishing and nature by joining scouting groups, 4-H, or other youth groups, by fishing at kids' fishing derbies, or by talking to the people who work in fishing shops.

Nobody knows everything there is to know about fishing. But the more you learn, the more respect you'll have for fish, for the outdoors, and for other people. And that makes having good fishing manners easy.

CHAPTER 9

Special Kinds of Fishing

ICE FISHING

The kinds of fishing you've already read about are great. But there are special fishing methods for special situations, and you might enjoy trying them.

When do you think is the best time of year for fishing? In summer the weather is hot, there's plenty of fish, you aren't busy going to school, and you can swim in the water. In fall the lakes are less crowded, and the tree colors are beautiful. Spring fishing lets you listen to birds, watch the snow melt, and get muddy. But winter might be the best fishing season of all. When you fish in winter, you don't need to cast, you don't need a boat, and the fish bite even when the lake is frozen.

In many places, lakes freeze solid on top. Fish still swim in the water beneath the ice, but the only way to catch those fish is by chopping a hole in the ice and fishing through it. That's called ice fishing, and in Canada and the northern United States, it's a fun sport all its own.

Fishing on ice can be dangerous, though. Don't fish alone or without permission. Make sure the ice is solid and several inches thick before you walk on it. Shorelines often have thin ice, and stepping in a hole in the ice can be dangerous.

Dress warmly for ice fishing. The outer layers of your clothing should be windproof and waterproof, and you should wear plenty of clothes underneath. Mittens are warmer than gloves, and a warm hat should be on every ice fisher's

Fishing in the winter, through the ice, is lots of fun.

head. Some people say ice fishing is the toughest way to fish, because you may feel like you're freezing. That's why warm clothing is so important.

Ice fishing requires some special equipment, but not much. To get to the fish, you can cut the top of the lake open with an ice drill or chop a hole with a long-handled chisel called a spud. Or you can find a hole that someone else drilled and left open. A scoop helps you catch the little chunks of ice that float around in a hole.

Ice fishing means fishing through a hole in the ice. If you use a short jigging rod, you might catch crappies like these.

There are two main ways to fish through the ice—with a short fishing rod, or with a tip-up. If you're used to summer fishing, you'll be surprised to know that, for winter, you probably want a shorter pole. Any size pole will work, but a short one works best because you can sit close to the hole and keep a close eye on the bobber. Two or three feet is about the right length for an ice fishing pole.

When ice anglers fish with bait, most of them add their bait to small lures. Fish are not as hungry when winter has made the water cold, so smaller baits and lures are used. The fish want something that's more like a snack and less like a meal.

Teardrop-shaped lures and ice flies (hooks with feathers wrapped around them) work for panfish. Any kind of bait will work, but wax worms and other grubs work the best. Using them, you can catch bluegills, crappies, and perch. Minnows—especially small ones—are good, too.

Bluegills bite in little pecks. Crappies are very tricky. When they feel your line being reeled in, they sometimes just let go and fall off the hook. Perch are delicious, and they're

Always dress warmly when you're ice fishing.

77

not too hard to catch. They like any kind of bait.

If you're fishing for panfish, start with your hook dangling right near the bottom of the lake. A little bobber helps you tell when a fish bites. Give it a tug and, if you feel a fish, pull in the line with your hands. You might need to pull your mittens off for a few minutes, so your fingers may get cold, but a bluegill or crappie flopping on the ice will make you feel warm again.

Walleyes, bass, and trout are sometimes caught by jiggling a spoon near the bottom. A short spinning rod with a spinning reel works well, and it lets you fight even a big fish.

A tip-up waves a flag at you when a fish bites.

Tip-ups are another way to fish through the ice. They hold a bait underwater and wave a flag at you when a fish bites. You don't have to hold the tip-up—you can even skate or have a snowball fight as long as you're close enough to run to the tip-up when a fish bites. Trout, northern pike, and walleyes are the top tip-up fish.

Trolling sometimes pays off with big fish that put up big fights.

TROLLING

Another kind of fishing—one that's used when the water is not frozen—is called trolling. Trolling means fishing with lures or plugs, but using a boat to pull the lures around the lake.

Trolling is especially popular on big lakes, where there's plenty of room to move around. Instead of casting, cranking in the lure, and waiting for a fish to strike, trollers let out the lure while a boat is moving slowly. Then they give the reel a crank or flip a lever, so that the fishing line stops going out. Because the boat is still moving, the lure follows, wobbling and gurgling in a fishy kind of way.

This big chinook salmon was caught by trolling in a large boat.

Sometimes that's all there is to trolling. At other times, you might use a downrigger—a cranking machine that makes sure the lure is deep, placed right where you want it.

When you're trolling, you really don't do much until a fish strikes. You can tell when that happens because the tip of your fishing rod will start bouncing like crazy. That usually means you're catching a salmon, a trout, a bass, a pike, or a walleye, and it's time to reel your fish in.

Trolling requires patience. But even on a day when the fish aren't biting, you get a fun boat ride and you can read or watch the scenery while you're waiting for a bite. When that bite comes, it's almost always a big fish that's been hunting for a meal.

FLY FISHING

Maybe you've heard of fly fishing. No, it doesn't mean fishing for flies. It's fishing *with* flies. Lures made of feathers, yarn, or fur are called flies. They're made to look like all sorts of buggy or fishy little creatures.

The biggest difference between fly fishing and the other kinds of fishing is the way casting is done. When you cast with a spinning or spin-cast rod, you toss the lure, and the fishing line follows the lure. But in fly fishing, you cast a heavier plastic line, and it carries the lure along with it.

Fly fishers sweep their fishing rods back and forth, and more line whizzes through the air with each sweep. When enough line is out, the caster sweeps the rod forward and points toward the spot where he wants the fly to land.

Some flies are made to look as much like a real insect as possible. Some of them float right on top of the water, while others act like sinking, swimming bugs. Some "flies" look like minnows, some like frogs, and some like creatures

Flies are light, and fly line is heavy. A fly fisher casts by whipping the line back and forth through the air. The fly is tugged along by the line.

nobody's ever seen! People have learned that certain fish will gobble up a certain kind of fly.

When a fish bites, there's either a tug on the line or a splash on the top of the lake or stream. Then the fight is on. Some people use the reel to fight the fish, while others like to tug the line in by hand, grabbing it just ahead of the reel.

Fly fishing is a challenging way to fish, since you have to learn how to cast, which flies to use, and how to win your fights with fish. But it sure makes you proud when you've learned all that—and caught a fish!

SALTWATER FISHING

Many of us do most of our fishing in freshwater, the water of rain and creeks and rivers and lakes. But if you live near an ocean, or visit one, you might fish in water that's called *saltwater* because it has salt dissolved in it. If you swim in the ocean and accidentally get a mouthful of water or lick your lips after swimming, you can taste the salt.

Fish that live in saltwater are different than those in freshwater. So is some of the equipment you use.

Salt makes metals such as iron and steel rust, and in a hurry. The ring guides on your fishing rod, parts of your reel, and even the hooks on your line lure can be damaged if you don't clean them properly. Some metals such as brass and stainless steel do not rust, and equipment for saltwater fishing is often made of them. Otherwise, you need to wash and dry your equipment after every outing.

Hooks, unless they're stainless steel, can simply be rinsed and dried. Reels should be rinsed, shaken to remove most of the water, and set aside to dry. Flush the rod guides with fresh, clean water, too. If your equipment was made

Saltwater equipment is made tough to protect it from salt, and heavy enough to handle big fish. These are saltwater trolling reels.

especially for saltwater fishing, you may not have to do all these things. Read the instructions that came with it.

People who fish in saltwater have something else to keep in mind besides equipment, weather, winds, and other things every angler thinks about. They keep track of the daily tides.

As the moon circles the earth, its gravity pulls on the earth. It pulls on the water of a big ocean, and the water follows it. When the moon's gravity is pulling on the ocean near you, the water level may be several feet lower. When the pull stops, the water goes back up.

Fishing is usually best at each spot at some time between high tide and low tide. Once you've learned which time is best for the fish you want to catch and the place where you're fishing, you can read the tide charts in your local newspaper. This will help you figure out when you should return to your favorite fishing spot.

There are three main ways to fish for saltwater fish. You can fish from the shore, often called the surf. You can fish from a pier, bridge, or dock. Or you can fish from a boat, pulling lures or bait behind a moving boat or fishing straight down from a boat that's held in place by a heavy anchor.

Saltwater fish move around a lot. If you're fishing from shore, a bridge, or a pier, you never know what you'll catch. It might be a Spanish mackerel, a cobia, or a jack crevalle.

Bluefish are especially popular among those who fish from the surf along the shoreline. These people wade into the water or cast from the beach. Bluefish can be caught at different places during different seasons, especially along the Atlantic Ocean coastline and the Gulf of Mexico.

The top fish is a small Spanish mackerel. The ones with the dark spots are spotted sea trout.

Tarpon put up great fights. People in small boats fish for tarpon in protected bays, and canals leading to the ocean are sometimes home to these fish.

Bonefish are also popular saltwater fish, especially in Florida, although they're found all along the Atlantic and Pacific ocean shorelines. They're relatives of tarpon.

In New England, anglers are always eager to catch striped bass. These bass come near the shore to attack smaller fish, so people can catch them right from shore. They put up great fights.

Snook are found in the southern United States. Some say a snook is a lot like a northern pike: When it decides to attack, it really attacks.

Many kinds of worms, fish and fish meat, and other natural items are used as bait for saltwater fish. It often takes a heavy lead weight to keep the bait on the bottom, and strong rods and reels to bring in the fish.

Special lead-head jigs, often baited with pieces of fish meat, work well on many saltwater fish.

Notice the sharp teeth of a Spanish Mackerel. Be careful if you handle one!

Cast out the jig and reel it back in slowly. Heavy spoons are good for fish that stay in deep water. Floating plugs trick some fish into swimming up to the surface for what looks like a meal. Try different spots and different reeling-in speeds, to see if you can find the right spot and speed for the fish that day.

You need to be careful with saltwater fish: Some have stingers, others have very sharp teeth. Some fish have more than one name, too, making it hard to learn which fish is which. So it's really important to fish in saltwater with an adult who knows about fish, how to catch them, and how to handle them.

Some of the biggest saltwater fish are caught by trolling. Blue sharks, swordfish, marlin, tuna, and others grow larger than adult humans, and very special equipment is needed to catch them.

Saltwater fish often strike harder and fight harder than freshwater fish. No matter what you catch—and you never know what you're going to catch in saltwater—you're in for a tussle!

FISHING AND LEARNING

You can learn more about all kinds of fish and fishing in books from the library, in magazines, from Scouts and other youth groups, at fishing tackle shops, and by entering fishing derbies. Everything you learn helps you have more fun and catch more fish. Someday you'll be proud to share what you've learned. You'll help somebody else become just what you love to be—a fisherkid!

Good luck!

CHAPTER 10

My Fishing Log

WHAT'S A FISHING LOG?

A log is like a diary or a journal. It's a place where you can write down things you do and things that happen. A *fishing* log is where you can write about your fishing trips. Use a page of the fishing log in this book to write about each trip. When you run out of pages, you can make another log in a notebook.

The fishing log can help you. If you caught a lot of fish on one trip using a certain kind of bait, maybe you want to fish at the same place again, using the same bait. On the other hand, if you *didn't* catch a lot of fish, maybe you wouldn't want to repeat the same trip or use the same bait. Either way, the fishing log will help you make your fishing plans.

Better yet, it helps you remember your very own fishing stories.

My Fishing Log

The date I went fishing was: _____

Here are the people I fished with: _____

Here's where I fished: _____

Here's the kind of bait or lures I used: _____

_____

Here's what the weather was like: _____

I fished at this time of day: _____

I caught this many fish: _____

Here's how big the fish were: _____

_____

The kinds of fish I caught were: _____

_____

Did I keep the fish or release them? _____

Here's what I saw besides fish: _____

_____

Here's what I did besides fishing: _____

_____

_____

Here's what I learned about fishing at this fishing spot: _____

_____

This fishing trip was: ☐ Great ☐ Pretty good ☐ Okay ☐ Not too good

My Fishing Log

The date I went fishing was: _____

Here are the people I fished with: _____

Here's where I fished: _____

Here's the kind of bait or lures I used: _____

_____

Here's what the weather was like: _____

I fished at this time of day: _____

I caught this many fish: _____

Here's how big the fish were: _____

_____

The kinds of fish I caught were: _____

_____

Did I keep the fish or release them? _____

Here's what I saw besides fish: _____

_____

Here's what I did besides fishing: _____

_____

_____

Here's what I learned about fishing at this fishing spot: _____

_____

This fishing trip was: ☐ Great   ☐ Pretty good   ☐ Okay   ☐ Not too good

My Fishing Log

The date I went fishing was: _____

Here are the people I fished with: _____

Here's where I fished: _____

Here's the kind of bait or lures I used: _____

_____

Here's what the weather was like: _____

I fished at this time of day: _____

I caught this many fish: _____

Here's how big the fish were: _____

_____

The kinds of fish I caught were: _____

_____

Did I keep the fish or release them? _____

Here's what I saw besides fish: _____

_____

Here's what I did besides fishing: _____

_____

_____

Here's what I learned about fishing at this fishing spot: _____

_____

This fishing trip was: ☐ Great   ☐ Pretty good   ☐ Okay   ☐ Not too good

My Fishing Log

The date I went fishing was: _____

Here are the people I fished with: _____

Here's where I fished: _____

Here's the kind of bait or lures I used: _____

_____

Here's what the weather was like: _____

I fished at this time of day: _____

I caught this many fish: _____

Here's how big the fish were: _____

_____

The kinds of fish I caught were: _____

_____

Did I keep the fish or release them? _____

Here's what I saw besides fish: _____

_____

Here's what I did besides fishing: _____

_____

_____

Here's what I learned about fishing at this fishing spot: _____

_____

This fishing trip was: ☐ Great ☐ Pretty good ☐ Okay ☐ Not too good

My Fishing Log

The date I went fishing was: _____

Here are the people I fished with: _____

Here's where I fished: _____

Here's the kind of bait or lures I used: _____

_____

Here's what the weather was like: _____

I fished at this time of day: _____

I caught this many fish: _____

Here's how big the fish were: _____

_____

The kinds of fish I caught were: _____

_____

Did I keep the fish or release them? _____

Here's what I saw besides fish: _____

_____

Here's what I did besides fishing: _____

_____

_____

Here's what I learned about fishing at this fishing spot: _____

_____

This fishing trip was: ☐ Great   ☐ Pretty good   ☐ Okay   ☐ Not too good

My Fishing Log

The date I went fishing was: _____

Here are the people I fished with: _____

Here's where I fished: _____

Here's the kind of bait or lures I used: _____

_____

Here's what the weather was like: _____

I fished at this time of day: _____

I caught this many fish: _____

Here's how big the fish were: _____

_____

The kinds of fish I caught were: _____

_____

Did I keep the fish or release them? _____

Here's what I saw besides fish: _____

_____

Here's what I did besides fishing: _____

_____

_____

Here's what I learned about fishing at this fishing spot: _____

_____

This fishing trip was: ☐ Great   ☐ Pretty good   ☐ Okay   ☐ Not too good

My Fishing Log

The date I went fishing was: _____

Here are the people I fished with: _____

Here's where I fished: _____

Here's the kind of bait or lures I used: _____

_____

Here's what the weather was like: _____

I fished at this time of day: _____

I caught this many fish: _____

Here's how big the fish were: _____

_____

The kinds of fish I caught were: _____

_____

Did I keep the fish or release them? _____

Here's what I saw besides fish: _____

_____

Here's what I did besides fishing: _____

_____

_____

Here's what I learned about fishing at this fishing spot: _____

_____

This fishing trip was: ☐ Great   ☐ Pretty good   ☐ Okay   ☐ Not too good

My Fishing Log

The date I went fishing was: _____

Here are the people I fished with: _____

Here's where I fished: _____

Here's the kind of bait or lures I used: _____

_____

Here's what the weather was like: _____

I fished at this time of day: _____

I caught this many fish: _____

Here's how big the fish were: _____

_____

The kinds of fish I caught were: _____

_____

Did I keep the fish or release them? _____

Here's what I saw besides fish: _____

_____

Here's what I did besides fishing: _____

_____

_____

Here's what I learned about fishing at this fishing spot: _____

_____

This fishing trip was: ☐ Great   ☐ Pretty good   ☐ Okay   ☐ Not too good